Mother Teresa

John Barraclough

First published in Great Britain by Heinemann Library
Halley Court, Jordan Hill, Oxford OX2 8EJ,
a division of Reed Educational and Professional Publishing Ltd.

OXFORD FLORENCE PRAGUE MADRID ATHENS
MELBOURNE AUCKLAND KUALA LUMPUR SINGAPORE TOKYO
IBADAN NAIROBI KAMPALA JOHANNESBURG GABORONE
PORTSMOUTH NH (USA) CHICAGO MEXICO CITY SAO PAULO

Designed by Ken Vail Graphic Design, Cambridge
Illustrations by Barbra Lofthouse
Printed and bound in Hong Kong / China

01
10 9 8 7 6 5 4 3

ISBN 0 431 02466 9

Some words are shown in bold, **like this**.
You can find out what they mean by looking
in the glossary. The glossary also helps you
say difficult words.

British Library Cataloguing in Publication Data

Barraclough, John
Mother Teresa. - (Lives & times)
1. Teresa, Mother, 1910 - Juvenile literature
2. Women missionaries - India - Biography - Juvenile literature
I. Title
266.2'092

Acknowledgements
The Publishers would like to thank the following for permission to reproduce photographs:
Andes Press Agency / Carlos Reyes – Manzo, p. 19; Camera Press Ltd / S.K. Dutt, pp. 17,18, 22

Cover photograph: Popperfoto

Our thanks to Betty Root for her comments in the preparation of this book.

Every effort has been made to contact copyright holders of any material reproduced in this book.
Any omissions will be rectified in subsequent printings if notice is given to the Publisher.

Contents

The first part of this book tells you the story of Mother Teresa.
The second part tells you how we can find out about her life.

Early life

Mother Teresa was born in 1910 in Albania. At that time she was called Agnes **Bejaxhiu**. When she was a little girl, Agnes talked to many **missionaries**. She wanted to help people.

When she was 18, Agnes became a **nun**. She was called Sister Teresa. She went to India to teach. She loved her work. But it upset her that so many people lived in **slums**.

First clinic and school

Teresa felt that God wanted her to help. She left the girls' school where she was working. She started a very simple **clinic** where she could help sick people from the **slums**.

The children who lived in the slums had no schools to go to. Teresa started to teach them in the street. She scratched the letters of the alphabet in the dust with a stick.

Mother Teresa's nuns

Two years later, Teresa asked some other **nuns** to work with her. Her name became Mother Teresa. All the nuns wore blue and white robes, like long, simple dresses.

One day, Mother Teresa found a dying woman in the street. She begged the hospital to let the homeless woman in. Otherwise the woman would have died out in the street.

A home for the dying

Mother Teresa knew that she had to do something to help the poor people who had no one to care for them when they were sick. Nobody should have to die in the street.

In 1952, Mother Teresa opened a home for the **destitute** and dying. The home was called **Kalighat**. Anyone was welcome here, and everyone was cared for.

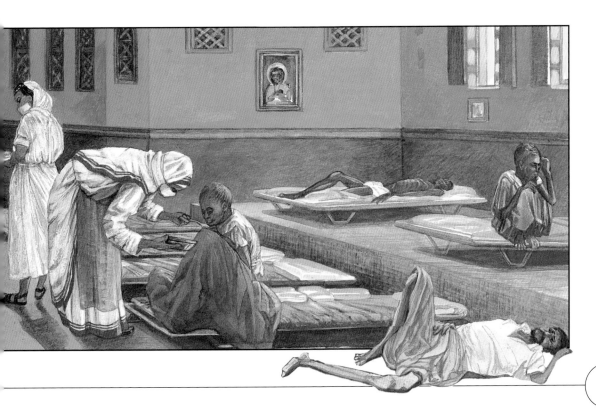

Children

Mother Teresa always cared deeply for everyone. She looked after many children whose parents could not look after them.

She and her **nuns** opened a children's
home called **Shishu Bavan**. All children
can go there and be cared for. No matter
how full it is, the nuns say, 'There is always
room for one more.'

Lepers

Lepers are people who have a serious disease called **leprosy**. Many lepers are thrown out of their homes. Mother Teresa provided a home for lepers in India.

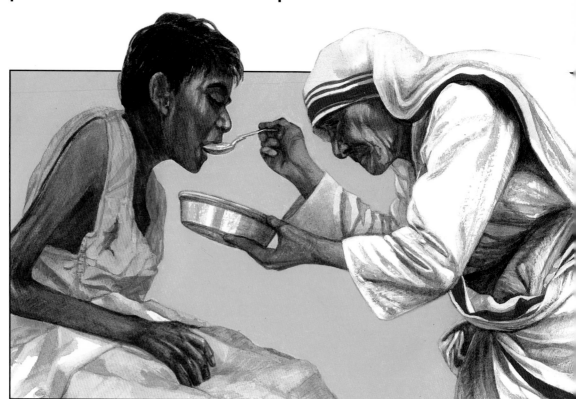

Prizes

Mother Teresa is famous for her work with homeless children and people who are ill and very poor. In 1979, she got an important prize, called the **Nobel Peace Prize**. This was to thank her for her work.

Photographs

When Mother Teresa left home to become a **nun** in India, she gave this photograph of herself to her aunt. It shows what she looked like as a young woman.

Mother Teresa worked with poor and ill people in many places. Her name is known everywhere. There are many photographs of her doing her work.

Many photographers have visited Mother Teresa's homes. This is a picture of her **nuns** giving out food.

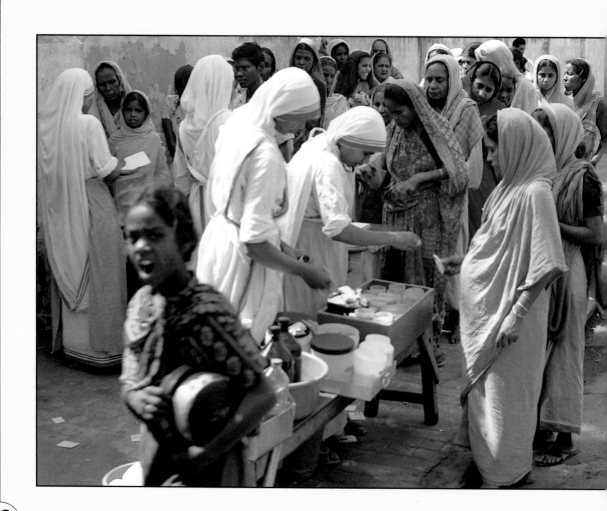

Mother Teresa worked a lot in India.
She also worked in about 100 other
countries. This photo shows her visiting
children in London.

Scrapbooks and letters

Mother Teresa's friend, Father Henry, kept a scrapbook. It tells us about Mother Teresa. On 16 August 1948, he wrote that Mother Teresa wanted to work with poor people in **Calcutta**.

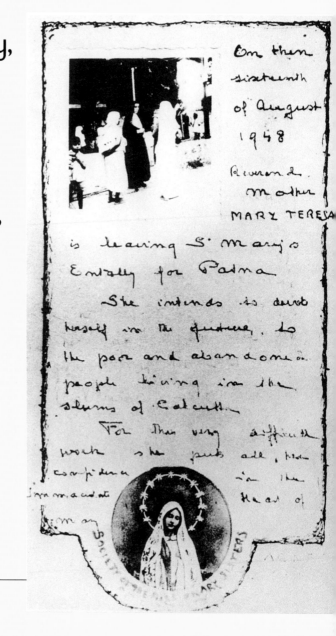

L.D.M.

MISSIONARIES OF CHARITY.
54-A, Lower Circular Road,
Calcutta _____ 195 .

My dear Mark Thank you for your gift. Love Jesus and Mary God bless You & Your Sister and little Baby

M. Teresa.

Mother Teresa wrote many thank-you letters to people who helped with her work. This one is to a charity that helps people with **leprosy**.

Signs and stamps

Kalighat, the home for people who are very poor and ill or dying, is also called Nirmal Hriday. This means the Place of the Pure Heart. The sign you can see here is by the entrance to the home.

When Mother Teresa got the **Nobel Peace Prize**, the Indian post office made this special stamp. It was a way of thanking her.

Glossary

This glossary explains difficult words, and helps you to say words which may be hard to say.

Bejaxhiu you say *beh-sha-shoo*

Calcutta a big city in India. You say *kal-KUH-ta*

clinic place where you go to see a nurse or doctor

destitute very poor

Kalighat home that Mother Teresa opened. You say *ka-lee-gat*

leper a person who has the disease leprosy. You say *leppa*

leprosy a skin disease

missionary person who travels to other countries to tell people about his or her religion. You say You say *mish-yun-erry*

Nobel Peace Prize prize that is given to people who have done something very special to help other people

nun woman who follows the Christian religion, and who lives as part of a group of nuns. They all follow the same rules. They pray, and often help other people

Shishu Bhavan you say *shi-shoo ba-van*

slums areas with very poor houses with no running water, electricity or gas. Often they are built from whatever people can find, such as spare wood, plastic and tin sheeting

Index